Josh Hamilton and Marin Hinkle in the WPA Theatre production of "Wonderful Time." Set design by Henry Dunn.

WONDERFUL TIME

BY JONATHAN MARC SHERMAN

★

DRAMATISTS
PLAY SERVICE
INC.

WONDERFUL TIME
Copyright © 1997, by Jonathan Marc Sherman

SPECIAL NOTE

Anyone receiving permission to produce WONDERFUL TIME is required (1) to give credit to the Author as sole and exclusive Author of the Play on the title page of all programs distributed in connection with performances of the Play and in all instances in which the title of the Play appears for purposes of advertising, publicizing or otherwise exploiting the Play and/or a production thereof. The name of the Author must appear on a separate line, in which no other name appears, immediately beneath the title and in size of type equal to 50% of the largest, most prominent letter used for the title of the Play. No person, firm or entity may receive credit larger or more prominent than that accorded the Author; and (2) to give the following acknowledgment on the title page of all programs distributed in connection with performances of the Play:

Originally produced by WPA Theatre
New York City, 1995
Kyle Renick, Artistic Director

SPECIAL NOTE ON SONGS, RECORDINGS, AND QUOTES

For performance of the songs, arrangements, recordings, or quotes mentioned in this Play that are protected by copyright, the permission of the copyright owners must be obtained; or other songs and recordings in the public domain substituted.

2

This one goes out to Eth and Josh,

brothers on the ride.

WONDERFUL TIME was produced by WPA Theatre (Kyle Renick, Artistic Director; Lori Sherman, Managing Director) in New York City on December 28, 1995. It was directed by Tim Vasen; the set design was by Henry Dunn; the costume design was by Mimi Maxmen; the lighting design was by Jeremy Stein; the sound design was by Aural Fixation; the dramaturg was Jill Rachel Morris; and the production stage manager was Gwendolyn D. Burrow. The cast was as follows:

LINUS WORTH ....Josh Hamilton
ROBIN; WAITRESS .... Anney Giobbe
ERNIE; PETER.. Silas Weir Mitchell
BETSY FLYNN .... Marin Hinkle
CLYDE .... Daniel Zelman

ACKNOWLEDGMENT

This play was written with support from Playwrights Horizons made possible in part by funds granted to the author through a commissioning program established by the Kathryn and Gilbert Miller Trust. The statements made and views expressed, however, are solely the responsibility of the author.

CHARACTERS

Linus Worth
Betsy Flynn
Clyde
Robin
Ernie
Peter
Waitress
Voices

NOTES

The action of the play takes place from a Friday to a Sunday in May. It starts on a university campus in California, travels to New York City, and ends up in Malibu Colony.

WONDERFUL TIME

SCENE ONE

A nondescript room. Linus Worth sits against a bland background. He is sort of good looking, sometimes charming, always lost. He is interviewed by an offstage Voice.

VOICE 1. Name.
LINUS. Linus Worth.
VOICE 1. Age.
LINUS. 23.
VOICE 1. Height. *(Linus answers.)* Weight. *(Linus answers.)* Eyes. *(Linus answers.)* Hair. *(Linus answers.)* Race.
LINUS. I shouldn't have to answer that.
VOICE 1. It's an optional question.
LINUS. It's optional?
VOICE 1. Yes.
LINUS. I didn't know that. Ask me again.
VOICE 1. Race.
LINUS. Marathon.
VOICE 1. Occupation.
LINUS. Film student.
VOICE 1. Drugs.
LINUS. Confusion.
VOICE 1. Alcohol.
LINUS. Confusion.
VOICE 1. Music.
LINUS. Makes the heart grow fonder.
VOICE 1. That's absence. Absence makes the heart grow fonder.
LINUS. Yeah, the absence of music makes the heart grow

fonder. In other words, I'm fond of music. *(Beat.)* I like music. *(Beat.)* I have some CDs.
VOICE 1.   Compact discs?
LINUS.   No, certificates of deposit. From my grandparents.
VOICE 1.   Sex.
LINUS.   Confusion.
VOICE 1.   Male or female?
LINUS.   Confusion.
VOICE 1.   Life.
LINUS.   Uhh … confusion.

SCENE TWO

Linus' dormitory room. On the wall by the bed is the famous Robert Doisneau poster "Le Baiser De L'Hotel DeVille, Paris 1950," with a man kissing a woman as people walk by. Linus sits on his bed with Robin, his girlfriend. They are in the middle of a conversation.

LINUS.   That *is* a bizarre dream. *(Beat.)* Was Miss New York a finalist?
ROBIN.   Have you been with anybody else?
LINUS.   *(Beat.)* "Been with"? What, you mean —
ROBIN.   Have you kissed or fooled around with or slept with somebody else? Have you been unfaithful? Have you cheated on me? You know, "been with."
LINUS.   … Yeah.
ROBIN.   *(Beat.)* What?
LINUS.   *Yeah.* I have been. Yeah.
ROBIN.   *(Stops smiling.)* With who?
LINUS.   Different people.
ROBIN.   *What* different people? Specifically.
LINUS.   All sorts of specific different people.
ROBIN.   It sounds like a lot.
LINUS.   Yeah.

ROBIN. *(Beat.) Why?*

LINUS. Well —

ROBIN. I'm not good enough?

LINUS. Robin, that's not it at all —

ROBIN. Are they better in bed?

LINUS. Robin —

ROBIN. I hope so. I really do. I hope you're not losing me over a bunch of *amateurs.*

LINUS. Losing you?

ROBIN. Losing me.

LINUS. *Why?*

ROBIN. I don't know. Maybe because you're a cheating liar, and a lying *cheat.*

LINUS. I never lied to you —

ROBIN. You never told me the truth.

LINUS. You can't walk out *now.*

ROBIN. I *can't?*

LINUS. What about Clyde's wedding?

ROBIN. I'm not going. *(The phone rings. Linus answers it.)*

LINUS. Yeah?... Hey, Clyde.

ROBIN. I'm going. *(Linus stands and blocks the door.)*

LINUS. Nothing, we're just getting ready for the trip.

ROBIN. Get away from the door, Linus.

LINUS. Robin's excited to meet you, too.

ROBIN. I'll scream.

LINUS. Yeah, I know. *(Robin screams.)* Primal *scream* thing ... releases tension. *(Robin screams again.)* Clyde, buddy, gotta go, see you soon, *later. (Linus hangs up the phone.)* Robin, we've been planning this trip for so long.

ROBIN. Get away from that door.

LINUS. I told everybody back home all about you.

ROBIN. Tell them a little bit more. Tell them I left you. Tell them you're an unfaithful prick. Tell them whatever you want to tell them, just get away from that door, you macho, macho shithead.

LINUS. One *macho* would be fine.

ROBIN. Don't try to turn this into a lesson, you stupid, stupid fuck. Yes, I needed to say *stupid* twice to illustrate the depths of your stupidity. One stupid just would not do.

LINUS. I'm not stupid —

ROBIN. Get away from that door.

LINUS. Okay, Robin, okay, you were right, those other girls — *amateurs.* You want comparison? Okay. Those girls are Snickers bars, you're a steak. They're quick fixes that tide me over until dinner time. You're the main course. Just, please, can't you wait until *after* the wedding to leave me? *(Robin starts to cry.)*

ROBIN. They're ... Snickers bars?

LINUS. Yeah — what's the matter?

ROBIN. And I'm a steak?

LINUS. Prime rib. Filet mignon What's wrong?

ROBIN. Snickers bars are sweeter than steak. Is that what you're saying? Is that what you mean?

LINUS. Robin —

ROBIN. You think I'm not sweet enough. Snickers bars are sweeter than steak.

LINUS. Snickers bars give you cavities.

ROBIN. Snickers bars are *satisfying,* right? Do those other girls *satisfy* you?

LINUS. Come on, Robin —

ROBIN. Do they *taste* better than me? Huh? Do they?

LINUS. I can't believe I got us talking about *food.*

ROBIN. They're sweeter, more satisfying, and taste better —

LINUS. They're just one night stands, Robin —

ROBIN. It adds up, Linus. Seven one night stands make a week. Three-hundred-sixty-five one night stands make a year.

LINUS. You overestimate me.

ROBIN. No, I don't, not anymore I don't. I'm going.

LINUS. What about the wedding?

ROBIN. Take a Snickers bar.

LINUS. I don't *want* to, I *want* —

ROBIN. I want you to get away from that door.

LINUS. I don't think you should leave like this — *(Robin tears down half of the Doisneau poster from the wall.)* What are you *doing?*

ROBIN. Getting you away from that door. *(Linus moves away from the door and walks towards the poster.)*

10

LINUS. This poster is *ruined.*

ROBIN. *We're* ruined, Linus.

LINUS. No, but, I mean, this is *really* ruined.

ROBIN. You wouldn't get away from that door. I told you, but you wouldn't move.

LINUS. I — I don't want you to go, Robin.

ROBIN. I'm going.

LINUS. Maybe I'll change.

ROBIN. Maybe. *(Beat.)* Bye. *(Robin walks out, closing the door behind her. Linus flops down onto the bed, in between the two halves of the poster: the man's half, which still hangs on the wall by the bed, and the woman's half, which is on the floor.)*

SCENE THREE

An editing room. Linus and Ernie watch images on the viewing screen of a flat bed editing machine. Ernie is a film student like Linus, and he's editing Linus' film. Linus seems edgy, Ernie seems distant.

ERNIE. That's it.

LINUS. That's all the generic footage we have?

ERNIE. Yup.

LINUS. We don't have more airplanes taking off?

ERNIE. That's all she wrote.

LINUS. Well, none of it really lifted my spirits. None of it made me soar alongside the plane.

ERNIE. It's all we got.

LINUS. But it's so *clichéd,* the plane-taking-off thing. It's gonna look like every other movie in the world.

ERNIE. What should we do, get some footage of a kid riding on a Big Wheel? It's a *plane* scene, Linus, the scene takes place on an airplane, and the easiest way to establish that is to *show* a plane taking off. That's why people *use* these shots, because they're easy.

LINUS.   Easy is for two o'clock in the morning at some party after you've had eight beers. Now is not the time for easy.

ERNIE.   What's wrong?

LINUS.   Nothing's wrong.

ERNIE.   What's wrong?

LINUS.   *Everything. (Beat.)* Do you ever feel like you're about to explode? I feel like I'm about to explode.

ERNIE.   Linus, you're a smart young guy living in a confusing technological maze of fear and pain. You're *supposed* to feel a little lost. That's *normal.*

LINUS.   No, not lost. I really feel like I'm about to *explode.* Literally. I mean ... *BOOM.* I'm twenty-three years old, you know, *BOOM,* all of a sudden my oldest friend is getting married and it's time to grow up.

ERNIE.   Growing up's great, you can go to bed whenever you want.

LINUS.   I have to get my life straight, figure everything out, get it in order and move along towards a happy future, right?

ERNIE.   That would be nice.

LINUS.   But how can I *do* that? I don't understand *anything.*

ERNIE.   You understand movies.

LINUS.   Fine, I understand movies, sort of. But I don't understand women or love or sex or truth or my friends —

ERNIE.   Or my family or work or society or technology or then or now or later or any of it, I know, I know, I know. You understand *nothing.* But don't let that prevent you from having a wild skateboard ride through this huge translucent spider we call *life.*

LINUS.   *(Beat.)* Are you *on* something?

ERNIE.   Not really. I'm just 'shrooming.

LINUS.   You're *what?*

ERNIE.   'Shrooming. You know, I ate some magic mushrooms and I'm tripping my brains out. But I just gave you some good advice, and I don't want you to deny it.

LINUS.   You're editing my film ... while you're *tripping.* I've got to get out of California, *now.*

ERNIE.   You should get some good wedding footage.

LINUS. *Everybody* makes wedding films. *The Wedding Banquet* —

ERNIE. *Sixteen Candles* —

LINUS. *The Deer Hunter* —

ERNIE. *Betsy's Wedding* —

LINUS. *Diner* —

ERNIE. *The Marrying Man* —

LINUS. *The Godfather* —

ERNIE. *Splash* —

LINUS. *Wedding In <u>Blood</u>.*

ERNIE. Of *course* there are lots of weddings in films. All tragedies end in death, all comedies end in marriage.

LINUS. Death, marriage … what's the *difference?*

ERNIE. You are really *down*, man. Listen, take a Valium right before the plane takes off, wash it down with some Scotch, before you know it, you'll wake up three thousand miles away, totally refreshed, feeling like a newborn baby.

LINUS. I don't have a Valium.

ERNIE. I do.

LINUS. Of *course* you do. I'm going. Don't edit anything without me.

ERNIE. I'll be fine —

LINUS. Seriously. I'm leaving you with my film. Don't turn it into *Yellow Submarine.*

ERNIE. Have a nice trip.

LINUS. *You* are having a nice *trip, I* will be having a nice *flight.*

ERNIE. You get so *obsessive* and *specific* when it comes to words, *man.* Relax.

LINUS. My best friend's getting married, you're eating magic mushrooms and floating around Jupiter when you're supposed to be editing my film, my girlfriend dumped me and I don't have a date and my flight's only a couple of hours away, so this is not the time to relax, *man.*

ERNIE. Why'd Robin dump you?

LINUS. I don't know. *(Beat.)* Yes, I *do* kind of know, actually. I was unfaithful.

ERNIE. How'd you get caught?

LINUS.   She had a dream that I was kissing all the finalists in the Miss America pageant, so she asked me if I'd been with anybody else, and I said yes.

ERNIE.   *(Beat.)* Rewind, play that back again — she has some sort of *dream,* asks you if you've been fucking around, you say *what?*

LINUS.   Yeah.

ERNIE.   *Yeah?*

LINUS.   Yeah.

ERNIE.   Stupid, stupid, *dumb,* what are you, out of your *mind?* You don't say *yeah,* you say *no.* Just Say *No.* What were you thinking?

LINUS.   I was thinking I should tell the truth.

ERNIE.   Why would you want to do that? *Lie.* Everybody lies. Robin probably lied. Who has dreams about the Miss America contest? *Lie.* Fuck the truth. The truth *sucks.* That's why you make films. That's why I take mushrooms. The truth can suck my dick.

LINUS.   *(Beat.)* I gotta go.

ERNIE.   Have a wonderful time.

LINUS.   *(Beat.)* What'd you say?

ERNIE.   Have a wonderful time.

LINUS.   Why *wonderful?*

ERNIE.   Huh?

LINUS.   You always say *good.* Whenever I have to go some-place, you always say "Have a good time." Why should I have a wonderful time this time? What's different about today?

ERNIE.   Linus, man, listen: I'm *tripping.* All right? Understand that? You want to have a good time, all right, have that. You want to have a wonderful time, fine, have that. Just stop be-ing so harsh. You're really bumming me out.

LINUS.   I'm sorry, I'm just really ... not calm. I'm tense.

ERNIE.   If you're so tense, don't go to the wedding.

LINUS.   I *have* to go. I'm the best man. *(Linus walks out.)*

ERNIE.   *(Beat.)* Somebody's gotta be. *(Beat.) I'm* the best man *(Slaps his right cheek.)* No, *I'm* the best man *(Slaps his left cheek.)* I'm the best man *(Right cheek.)* No, I'm the best man *(Left cheek.)* I'll be the best man *(Right cheek.)* My hero! *(Left cheek.)* Curses — fuckshitfuckshit — Foiled again! *(Right cheek. Ernie continues to absently slap himself on the left cheek, then the right cheek, over and over.)*

SCENE FOUR

Linus walks along a path on the college campus, lost in thought, a backpack on his shoulder. He passes a female student with a video camera. She calls out to Linus. Her name is Betsy, and she's a lovely free spirit wearing a baby doll print dress with a long string of knotted pearls around her neck and wire sunglasses with blue frames on her eyes.

BETSY. Linus, right? *(Linus stops and turns to look at Betsy.)*
LINUS. Yeah?
BETSY. Quick: What's the most spontaneous thing you've ever done?
LINUS. What?
BETSY. Right, what's the most spontaneous thing you've ever done?
LINUS. Oh. *(Beat.)* Umm, well, *this.* Right now.
BETSY. Answering this question?
LINUS. No, well, you see, I haven't done it yet, I'm about to do it — *(Linus pulls out two plane tickets.)* You see these?
BETSY. Uh-huh. Look into the camera.
LINUS. Well, these are two round-trip plane tickets to New York City for the weekend. My best friend is getting married. I'm the best man. So, you know, obviously, one of these tickets is for me.
BETSY. Very spontaneous thing to do. New York for the weekend. Highly spontaneous.
LINUS. No, the spontaneous thing is that *this* ticket over here, that's yours. *(Linus hands one of the tickets to Betsy.)* And our flight is in one hour. *(Beat.)*

15

SCENE FIVE

Linus and Betsy are sitting next to one another on the airplane. Linus is sitting in the aisle seat. Betsy is next to the window. Betsy has a large purse on her shoulder and a copy of Rilke's Letters to a Young Poet *in her hand.*

BETSY. I was getting so fed up with all the boring things people were doing. It seemed like all the poetry had disappeared from daily life, nobody just *did* interesting things. Everything was just so planned and bland and self-indulgent. So I decided to do a class project exploring spontaneity among today's college students.

LINUS. At the risk of cliché, what's your major?

BETSY. American Studies.

LINUS. At the risk of asking too many questions —

BETSY. What's life without risk?

LINUS. If you're an American Studies major, why are you reading Rilke? He wasn't American the last time I checked.

BETSY. Sometimes, you need to take a break from something to be able to see it with fresh eyes.

LINUS. I said that to my girlfriend. She told me to stop trying to justify cheating.

BETSY. Girlfriend?

LINUS. Ex-girlfriend.

BETSY. Cheating?

LINUS. Yeah. Possibly ex-cheating. Possibly just a preview of things to come for the rest of my life. I *am* trying to improve —

BETSY. That's admirable.

LINUS. That's a baby doll dress, isn't it?

BETSY. This? Yeah. From Betsey Johnson.

LINUS. I have many weaknesses, and one of my weakest is for baby doll dresses. Let me correct that: for girls *in* baby doll dresses. Let me correct *that:* for *women* in baby doll dresses.

BETSY. I'm gonna need a more formal dress —

LINUS.   You can borrow one of my sister's. What else are you gonna need?

BETSY.   Shoes. Everything else I need is right here: toothbrush, skin cream, Valium —

LINUS.   Valium?

BETSY.   Sure. Thank God I have some. Six hour plane trips are not my idea of fun. Pop a Valium, wash it down with one of those little bottles of something, wake up when we get there. You should try it.

VOICE 2.   If you look towards the screen in the front of your cabin, we will now be showing a preview of our in-flight movie feature. *(Linus and Betsy watch the following movie preview, which the audience hears but doesn't see.)*

VOICE 3.   Gatorade Tarkington from the Dallas Cowboys is Romeo, a patriotic cop who's starting to lose hope.

ROMEO.   We're losing the streets to these drug lords, and I don't think there's a damn thing I can do about it ... with or without my motorized skateboard.

VOICE 3.   Fiona Drazzledorf from the Calvin Klein commercials is Juliet, a hooker with a heart of gold ... only her heart stopped beating last year.

JULIET.   I don't care *who* you are, God, you have to send me back down to Earth. My kid *needs* me.

VOICE 3.   There's never been an action-adventure-love-story quite like this one: *Romeo and Juliet and Guns.*

SCENE SIX

Linus and Betsy sit in the back of a limousine. Betsy is looking at the small bar.

BETSY.   You want something to drink?

LINUS.   *(Beat.)* No, thanks. *(Beat.)* Listen, Betsy, I'm gonna try something with you —

BETSY.   I *see.*

LINUS. No, that didn't sound right, I mean, I'm — I'd like to be totally honest with you.

BETSY. Totally honest?

LINUS. I want to tell the truth.

BETSY. The truth?

LINUS. Yeah. I thought I never lied to my ex-girlfriend, and she thought I never told the truth, so — you know, I think I should make sure I tell the truth. Rather than just being quiet. I think it's a good idea.

BETSY. Go right ahead.

LINUS. Let me start with something easy. I'm riding in a limo with you, your name is Betsy, my name is Linus.

BETSY. So far, so good.

LINUS. Now things get more complicated.

BETSY. Have you ever killed anybody?

LINUS. No.

BETSY. Just checking.

LINUS. I'm nervous around you.

BETSY. What did I do?

LINUS. It's not something you did, it's just who you *are*. I mean, we just flew across the nation together.

BETSY. Do you think we should get married?

LINUS. *(Horrified.) What?*

BETSY. I'm joking.

LINUS. Betsy, if you have to say "I'm joking" after a joke, chances are it's not really funny. We're going to a wedding tomorrow, it's not something to joke about.

BETSY. You just seem so *serious* all of a sudden.

LINUS. *(Beat.)* I didn't used to be the person I am now. *(Beat.)* I was — well, I was crazy for a while.

BETSY. What do you mean, crazy?

LINUS. I was ... different. It all kind of came to a boiling point when I had this date with Destiny.

BETSY. What kind of date with destiny?

LINUS. The kind where you take a hooker to the prom.

BETSY. Is this for real?

LINUS. I'll show you the prom pictures. I have them back home.

18

BETSY.   Couldn't you have asked a cheerleader?

LINUS.   I got really obsessed with going to the prom with a professional. It was my rebellious period. Long hair. Drugs. Drinking. But it didn't seem complete without a prostitute named Destiny as a prom date.

BETSY.   Her name wasn't really *Destiny*.

LINUS.   Destiny O'Toole. She said it was on her birth certificate. She was actually pretty sweet. But when I was, you know, *screwing* her —

BETSY.   You slept with her?

LINUS.   You buy a car, you drive it. There I was, I had created my own little scandal, I was wasted, I was on top of this woman, my hair was longer than her hair, and I thought of Jennifer.

BETSY.   Who's Jennifer?

LINUS.   Jennifer Karetnick. She was a friend of mine when I was a little kid, eight or nine years old, and I used to go over to her apartment to play. I'd tell my mother, "I'm going over to Jennifer's to play." Didn't know what we'd do. We didn't plan anything. We just set aside the afternoon to have fun. And, you know, we *did*. We always did. We found a way to enjoy ourselves. We didn't need any props or poses — it didn't have to be hip or cool or interesting, we just … *played*. I decided right there, on top of an Irish hooker named Destiny, I wanted to play again. Just play. *(Beat.)* I got my hair cut the next day.

BETSY.   I wrote Huey Lewis a fan letter.

LINUS.   That's not so bad.

BETSY.   I sent him my underwear.

LINUS.   That's bad.

BETSY.   I sent my underwear to every teen idol I could think of, praying my parents would get upset. And I *like* my parents.

LINUS.   Did they get upset?

BETSY.   No, they just kept buying me new underwear. I tried *everything*, anything to get them to pay attention, typical stuff, anything to shock the shit out of them. They kept trying to set me up with everybody's *son* — this twisted parade, a bunch of rich, handsome boys, all headed for success, marching towards our house with the Parental Seal of Approval. Boring as hell, incredibly predictable, always doing something to prove they weren't like everybody else, they were really *wacky* and *different*. It was so ... *precious*. I started going out with a guitar player who bit my breasts.

LINUS. He *bit* them? Are they *okay?*

BETSY. Oh, yeah, that part was great, but he stole my second favorite necklace, and that wasn't so great. He did make my parents really upset, though, so I guess it was worth it, in some twisted way.

LINUS. He got the job done.

BETSY. *Finishing* and *work* weren't really his specialties. But he was dynamite for our first two-and-a-half weeks. Those were undeniably great.

LINUS. They always are.

BETSY. Sure are.

LINUS. *(Pause.)* Do you think we were meant to mate for life?

BETSY. You and me?

LINUS. People in general. *(Beat.)* The average caveman only lived seventeen years, you know. *(Betsy laughs.)* It's true.

BETSY. Imagine an eight-and-a-half-year-old caveman having a mid-life crisis — divorcing his nine-year-old cavewife and dating a cavegirl half his age —

LINUS. *Four.* I mean, "Till death do us part" to a caveman is like saying "Till next week." But, you know, with things like modern dentistry keeping people alive until they're a hundred years old, it's a frightening commitment to make.

BETSY. You've given this one a lot of thought.

LINUS. I just broke up with my girlfriend. Actually, she broke up with me. Because I couldn't stay faithful. Yes, it's been on my mind. I'm really stressed. I just want to play spin-the-bottle.

BETSY. It might not be too suspenseful with just the two of us. We could ask the chauffeur —

LINUS. Do you like me at all?

BETSY. What?

LINUS. Do you think I'm cute or nice or funny or, I don't know, interesting, or anything remotely attractive, or was I just something spontaneous?

BETSY. *(Gentle, nice, quiet, serious, simple.)* I like you.

LINUS. I'm sorry to be so blunt, but I'm trying to be truthful, and I was wondering, and, you see, I kind of like you, too, I think, but the main reason I wanted you to come — I actually *really* like you, come to think of it, but the main reason I wanted you to come was absolute fear. *(Beat.)* And terror.

BETSY. You keep saying things like that, you keep getting tense and afraid and then we make some jokes and then you get tense and afraid again. Is it just going home? Is it going home with *me*? What is it?

LINUS. All of the things I did, back when I was crazy, before I cut my hair, all of the things I did, I did with Clyde. I did everything with Clyde. And he's getting married, and he's expecting me to come be his best man, and he's expecting to meet this wonderful young woman I told him about, and she broke up with me this morning.

BETSY. *This morning?*

LINUS. This morning.

BETSY. I didn't know that.

LINUS. That's because I didn't tell you. I mean, functionally, the relationship has been over for a while, but officially — 10:45 this morning ... Pacific Time ...

BETSY. Are you all right?

LINUS. Do I *seem* like I'm all right? No, actually, I'm *sort* of all right, but the prospect of facing my past alone would have made me not all that all right, so I asked you to come with me. *(Beat.)* And here you are.

BETSY. And here I am.

SCENE SEVEN

Linus' childhood bedroom, with a teddy bear on the bed. Linus and Betsy walk in.

BETSY. Where is everybody?

LINUS. Well, my little sister's a party queen, and my Dad

travels a lot ever since my Mom died. I think he's in Japan now.

BETSY. What's he doing in Japan?

LINUS. I'm not at liberty to say. *(Linus takes a photograph from the bookshelf and hands it to Betsy.)* This is my prom picture. *(Linus walks to the closet and takes out a tuxedo.)* This is my tux. *(Linus reaches into the jacket pocket and pulls out a business card.)* And this is Destiny's card. *(Betsy looks at the card.)*

BETSY. That's all? Just "Destiny"?

LINUS. It's her name *and* her phone number. *(Beat.)* 337-8469 ... D-E-S-T-I-N-Y.

BETSY. How convenient.

LINUS. I told you I wasn't making it up.

BETSY. You sure weren't. She's very pretty.

LINUS. I paid double. I figured, how many proms does a guy have? *(Beat.)* Umm, you can sleep in here, I'll sleep in my father's room.

BETSY. Okay.

LINUS. I'll go get some dresses from Sally's closet, so you can pick something out for tomorrow.

BETSY. Can I take a t-shirt or something to sleep in?

LINUS. What's mine is yours.

BETSY. You may regret that.

LINUS. Be right back. *(Linus walks out of the room. Betsy takes a T-shirt and boxer shorts from the closet, goes into the bathroom and shuts the door. After a few moments, Linus walks in and hangs five dresses on some hooks that hang on the wall. The bathroom door opens and Betsy walks out, wearing the t-shirt and boxer shorts. She's just washed her face.)* That shirt never looked like that when I wore it.

BETSY. A couple of silicone injections and you'd be a new woman, Linus.

LINUS. I brought you five to look at.

BETSY. Rainbow colors. Like Assorted Fruit Life Savers.

LINUS. That was the look I was going for. *(Betsy takes* Letters to a Young Poet *from her purse.)* You gonna read?

BETSY. I always read in bed. It puts me to sleep.

LINUS. I could read it to you, if you wanted.

BETSY. *(Beat.)* Sure. That'd be nice. *(Betsy flips on the lamp by the bed, turns off the main room light, and gets into bed. Linus walks over and sits on the edge of the bed. Betsy picks up the teddy bear.)* Does this bear have a name?

LINUS. Seymour the Bear. He's great for venting aggression. *(Linus throws the teddy bear across the room and it hits the wall.)* I've missed that bear.

BETSY. That's horrible.

LINUS. It's a stuffed animal. *(Linus opens the book.)* Now, let's see. *Letters to a Young Poet* — Letter Number Three: "Grow up and stop rhyming."

BETSY. It doesn't say that.

LINUS. I'm reading between the lines. You do it your way, I'll do it mine.

BETSY. Just read it.

LINUS. Let's see now ... *(Beat. Linus reads Betsy a bit of the third Letter* as the lights fade.)*

SCENE EIGHT

A banquet hall, where Clyde's wedding is taking place. Linus picks up a glass of water from the table. He taps a spoon against the glass a few times.

LINUS. Uhh, I'm told it's customary for the best man to make a toast, so ... Clyde was my first friend. We've got baby pictures together. We grew up together. I remember when we were ten, Clyde and I were bored one day and decided to go check out the Temple of Dendur at the Met. So there we are, and I'm about to throw a penny into the water surrounding the temple and make my wish, when Clyde hands me his skateboard to hold and says he has to wade through the water. He starts taking off his sneakers and his socks and I'm standing

---

* See Special Note on Quotes on copyright page.

next to him saying, "Clyde, you're crazy, you're gonna get in trouble, I'm staying right here." But he wouldn't listen. He said he had a big wish to make, too big for just a penny, he had to really use himself, really use his *whole self* for this one. Sure enough, when the coast was clear and no guards were in the room, Clyde walked through the wishing pool and got out on the other side. And the next day, he not only got his first kiss, but he got his second kiss as well, thereby beating me to female lips by approximately two years. *(Beat.)* And now, here we are, thirteen years later, and Clyde's getting married, and I'm supposed to make a toast because I'm the best man, and all I can say is ... you may be crazy, you may get in trouble, and, at least for the moment, I'm staying right where I am, but to you, Clyde, and to your beautiful bride, Jolie, may all your wishes come true. That's it, I'm done, everybody can go back to what they were doing.

SCENE NINE

Linus and Clyde are sitting at a table, talking passionately to one another, the way two old friends who haven't seen each other in way too long can do after they warm up. Clyde is a wealthy young beatnik, with a goatee and a Gold Card. He's wearing tails and sunglasses.

CLYDE.   Racism. Big issue. Massive. Lots of different angles. Tough to comprehend. I take little steps. Refuse to do my laundry. Eat Reese's peanut butter cups instead.
LINUS.   *What?*
CLYDE.   You see, I'm telling you, you overlook this kind of stuff. When you do your laundry, you're supposed to separate the colors from the whites, right? Well, there is no way I'm going to support something like that. Instead, I find comfort in a Reese's peanut butter cup. You got your chocolate in my peanut butter. No, you got your peanut butter on my choco-

late. At first, granted, it's a frightening concept, but you taste it and you realize combining different elements and tastes isn't such a bad idea.

LINUS. You just have your maid do your laundry.

CLYDE. That's beside the point. The point is there are important messages in unexpected places, and it's our duty to search for them.

LINUS. I do that with Good and Plenty. I always get them as a sort of model for my life. My desire for a balanced life. A life of Good and Plenty —

CLYDE. Too much candy isn't good for you. Eat some fruit.

LINUS. Good and Plenty. Moral and yet still an abundance of riches.

CLYDE. Riches or women?

LINUS. Yes. Both. Either. Yes.

CLYDE. I model my life after Apple Jack, the kid on the cereal box. Just an upside-down, happy kind of guy.

LINUS. But what about the reality behind the fantasy? Apple Jack falls on his head.

CLYDE. People *need* fantasy.

LINUS. I don't know. You buy a piece of Bazooka chewing gum, you read the comic, there's Bazooka Joe with a patch on his eye, and nobody ever says, "Hey, Bazooka Joe, remember that time when the spike went through your eye and you bled profusely? Wasn't that funny?"

CLYDE. I need a drink. *(Clyde finishes the drink on the table in front of him.)* I need another drink.

LINUS. You're drinking a lot.

CLYDE. You want a drink?

LINUS. I don't drink anymore, Clyde.

CLYDE. I'm sorry, I knew that. I'm sorry. I'm just used to you —

LINUS. I know.

CLYDE. I *do* want another drink. Come get one with me. You can get a Shirley Temple or something.

LINUS. You *are* the groom. *(Linus and Clyde get up. Clyde spots two half-finished drinks and stops.)*

CLYDE. Is the glass half-full or half-empty?... Find one of

each, mix them together — *(Clyde pours the drink in one of the glasses into the other glass and stirs it with his finger.)* Good stiff drink. *(Clyde drinks his concoction and walks off. Linus follows him.)*

SCENE TEN

The men's bathroom. Linus and Clyde walk in. Clyde is drinking a vodka cranberry, Linus is drinking a Shirley Temple.

CLYDE.   I *like* her, Linus, I really do, I think she's a good person. We laugh. I think she's smart, I like the way she looks when she wakes up. We have really good sex, you know? We laugh and sometimes we don't laugh, and ... I don't know, man, I guess, you know, I love her. Valentine's Day doesn't bug me, you know what I'm saying? *(Beat.)* Plus, it's a great reason to throw a party and wake up to adulthood real fast, right? Microwave coming-of-age. *(Beat.)* I really love her.

LINUS.   I really love catfish, but I don't want to eat it three meals a day for the rest of my life. I'm a Gemini, I can't choose just one thing. And I shouldn't have to. Four basic food groups, so why just one woman? Tell me that.

CLYDE.   Because women aren't food.

LINUS.   We evidently don't know the same people. I walk around campus at school, you know, it's really *hot*. The temperature's high. The girls don't wear a lot. And they look so delicious. You talk to them, at a party, or a class, or the cafeteria, you know, and they *sound* tasty —

CLYDE.   They *sound* tasty?

LINUS.   They sound *tasty*. It's like this buffet of women. There's so *many* of them.

CLYDE.   There's a lot of extraordinary women in this world.

LINUS.   I *know*. I had this twisted dream the other night: Three ménage à trois — a ménage à trois of ménage à trois. A triangle, two women on each point, me smack dab in the middle. Diana Ross and Farrah Fawcett were over there,

Audrey Hepburn and Vivien Leigh were over there, Marcia Brady and Rosalynn Carter were over there —

CLYDE. Rosalynn Carter?

LINUS. Hottest first lady *ever*…. Six older women and me. It was — it just … *was. (Beat.)* I love older women, except how do you pick them up? What do you say? "Remember Watergate? I don't." *(Clyde finishes the drink he was holding and pulls a pack of rolling papers and a small bag of marijuana from one of his pockets. He starts rolling a joint. Pause.)* You know, from an evolutionary standpoint, it makes sense for men to fuck around. Biologically, I mean.

CLYDE. Where the fuck did that come from?

LINUS. It's just stuff that's been on my mind.

CLYDE. Just because something's been on your mind doesn't mean you can use Darwin to justify your sex life.

LINUS. I'm serious. Monogamy makes more sense for women. For women, the focus is quality. For men: quantity.

CLYDE. I can't believe you really *are* using Darwin to justify your sex life! Linus, I'm shocked.

LINUS. I'm serious.

CLYDE. I'm aware of that. Listen, you can justify your point-of-view, and I can justify mine. I've got somebody who I know, who I care about. I know stories about her childhood. Why would I want to go through all the getting-to-know-somebody stuff again?

LINUS. Because that can be the best part. I love the mystery, the excitement of getting to know somebody new, exploring their body for the first time, getting used to the way their skin tastes, not knowing who they are, just knowing you want to be together.

CLYDE. Sounds very *Last Tango in Paris* to me.

LINUS. Exactly. I love that movie. "No names, everything outside this room is bullshit." Exactly. That's what I love.

CLYDE. May I remind you what happens at the end of *Last Tango in Paris*, Linus? Shall I refresh your memory? The lady *kills* the guy. He gets *killed* at the end. *(Clyde turns and speaks directly to the audience.)* Sorry if I spoiled the movie for you, folks, but come on, already, you should have seen it.

SCENE ELEVEN

The banquet hall. Betsy is sitting alone at a table. Peter, an attractive guy the same age as Linus and Clyde, sits down next to her.

PETER.   People are starting to talk.

BETSY.   What about?

PETER.   You sitting here all alone. They say you're in love with yourself. Tell me it's not true.

BETSY.   *(Knowingly.)* Ah, ha.... If you don't love yourself, how can you begin to love anybody or anything else?

PETER.   Touché. *(Beat.)* I don't think I've ever seen you before.

BETSY.   I *know* I've never seen you before.

PETER.   Are you a friend of the bride?

BETSY.   No, I'm with a friend of the groom.

PETER.   I'm a friend of the groom, but you're not with me, which makes me think you must be with a different friend of the groom.

BETSY.   Sherlock Holmes, move out of the way.

PETER.   Who's your friend?

BETSY.   Linus Worth.

PETER.   Oh, *God.* You're — you must be Robin. All of us have heard about you for so long. You know, I grew up with Linus —

BETSY.   Betsy.

PETER.   Excuse me?

BETSY.   My name's Betsy. I'm not Robin, I'm Betsy.

PETER.   Oh, I'm sorry.

BETSY.   Nice to meet you.

PETER.   My name's Peter.

BETSY.   Nice to meet you, Peter.

PETER.   Nice to meet you, *Betsy.* I just thought — you know, that Linus was coming with *Robin* ...

BETSY.   They broke up yesterday.

PETER.   Oh. That's too bad. Well, good ol' Linus, sort of a Superman that way, faster than a speeding bullet, getting right back on the proverbial horse and all ...

BETSY.   I don't mean to burst your bubble or whatever, but Linus and I haven't even so much as kissed one another.

PETER.   Oh, I see. Just friends?

BETSY.   We just met, actually. Yesterday.

PETER.   He didn't — he didn't, by any chance, *hire* you?

BETSY.   Are you asking if I'm a *whore?*

PETER.   Well, I just — it's just that, at our prom —

BETSY.   No, I'm not a professional. I go to school with Linus. We hang out with different people, but I saw this film he made —

PETER.   How are his films? All of us back here are always trying to make him send something along, a videotape or something, but — what's his stuff *like?* What's it *about?*

BETSY.   Well, the one I saw, they were showing a bunch of student films and Linus showed his, this short film called *First Kiss. (Beat.)* It starts off late one afternoon on this empty beach, and this boy drives up in a big truck with a friend. They start taking things from the back of the truck. An enormous brass bed and beautiful bedding. *(Beat.)* Then, there are these two poles with some canvas stretched between them. They secure the poles in the water, so there's a small movie screen a little ways off the shore. It keeps getting a little darker, bit by bit. *(Beat.)* They take a stand from the truck and put it behind the brass bed, then put a film projector on the stand, and, by now, the moon is rising, this full, shining, beautiful, perfect moon. *(Beat.)* The friend gets into the truck and drives off, while the boy puts some film into the projector, makes sure nobody comes along to ruin anything, and adjusts everything *just so. (Beat.)* Finally, the truck comes back, and the door opens. And out walks this girl, who sees the boy, and the bed, and the moon, and the makeshift movie theater. *(Beat.)* And she smiles. *(Beat.)* So, they get on the bed, and the movie starts. *Willy Wonka.* And they kiss, for the first time. And they just keep kissing, as if none of it was planned, all of it just happened, this one moment just ... *was.*

PETER.   *(Beat.)* That reminds me of this film I saw when I was in Paris my junior year ...

29

SCENE TWELVE

The men's bathroom. Linus and Clyde are standing in front of the bathroom mirror. Clyde is smoking a joint.

LINUS.   And she asked me if I had been unfaithful. And I told her the truth. *(Beat.)* I'm so confused.

CLYDE.   *(Offering his joint.)* You want a hit?

LINUS.   *(Beat.)* No. I just want to be *not* confused.

CLYDE.   You *sure* you don't want a hit?

LINUS.   Why do you still smoke that stuff?

CLYDE.   *(Beat.)* You know …

LINUS.   I want to hear what you have to say.

CLYDE.   To alleviate boredom.

LINUS.   Clyde, if you have to alleviate boredom at your own wedding, you may be in some serious trouble.

CLYDE.   It calms me down. I mean, who knows if this is even *real?* You know? Maybe we're not in control of our own lives anyway. Maybe we're elaborate puppets, this mirror is a camera, there's an audience of people, or an audience of *beings,* and they're out there, watching us, watching what we do. So what if I get married or don't get married, you know, in the end, in the long run, we're born, we fuck, we die.

LINUS.   You're baked.

CLYDE.   I'm married and I'm drunk and I want to go on my honeymoon and *bone.*

LINUS.   We've been away from the party so long, your wife probably ran off with the bandleader.

CLYDE.   Hug me.

LINUS.   Why?

CLYDE.   Because I love you, you fuck. *(Linus hugs Clyde.)* I love you, man.

LINUS.   Same here, buddy. *(Clyde breaks from the hug.)*

CLYDE.   All right, I got a honeymoon to get on with. *(Clyde stubs out the joint on one of the sinks. He takes out some Visine and Binaca, puts some Visine in his eyes, and sprays Binaca in his*

mouth.) Over and — *(Pause. Clyde stares at Linus.)*
LINUS.   Oh, umm … *out. (They exit the bathroom.)*

SCENE THIRTEEN

The banquet hall. Betsy and Peter are sitting at the table. Linus walks over.

LINUS.   Hey, Peter.

PETER.   Hey, Linus. Betsy here was just telling me about the stuff you're doing out on the West Coast. Sounds great.

LINUS.   Actually, no, it doesn't sound great, 'cause all I've made are silent films so far. But when I make one that *does* sound great, you'll be the first to know.

PETER.   Awww, same ol' Linus, always kidding.

LINUS.   Yeah, you obnoxious piece of boring shit.

PETER.   *(Beat.)* Excuse me?

LINUS.   You know me, same ol' Linus, always kidding.

PETER.   *Right.* Well, Betsy, it's been a pleasure. Excuse me. *(Peter walks away. Linus sits in his chair.)*

BETSY.   That wasn't very nice.

LINUS.   That guy's been a prick since he was seven.

BETSY.   At least he's consistent.

LINUS.   Did he have anything interesting to say?

BETSY.   He talked to me, which is more than I can say for you.

LINUS.   I'm talking to you.

BETSY.   Where have you been for the past forty-five minutes?

LINUS.   I was with Clyde. We were talking.

BETSY.   I was about to call the police and report you as kidnapped.

LINUS.   What if I said I was sorry?

BETSY.   Depends if that's an apology or a description.

LINUS.   Both.

31

BETSY. I'd say actions speak louder than words.

LINUS. You shouldn't have to *say* actions speak louder than words. You should *act* actions speak louder than words. *(Betsy is not amused.)* Okay, okay, okay. What if I show you the best time of your life tonight? Spontaneity at its finest. We'll paint the town red.

BETSY. I'd say red is my favorite color. *(Linus pulls the cherry out of his Shirley Temple and hands it to Betsy.)*

LINUS. Here.

BETSY. Thanks. *(Betsy eats the cherry, holding the stem.)* You're wondering if I can knot this stem with my tongue, aren't you?

LINUS. Yeah.

BETSY. Keep wondering. *(Betsy tosses the cherry stem away.)*

LINUS. What'd you and Peter talk about?

BETSY. We just kissed a lot.

LINUS. Oh, really?

BETSY. No. We mostly talked about you, actually.

LINUS. Oh, no, what'd he say?

BETSY. I said more than he did. I told him about *First Kiss*.

LINUS. My *film First Kiss?*

BETSY. Yeah.

LINUS. You *saw* that?

BETSY. Yeah. Last year.

LINUS. What'd you think?

BETSY. I don't think I'd be here with you if I hated it.

LINUS. So, things are not as spontaneous as they seem.

BETSY. Maybe not, maybe so.

LINUS. I have a confession to make. I sort of knew you, too.

BETSY. How?

LINUS. I saw you once at a party.

BETSY. Oh, that doesn't count.

LINUS. I remember it very well. I looked across the room, and I spotted some pearls, which you don't see everyday these days, so I looked up to see who was wearing them, and there you were, and you were talking to somebody, just smiling and laughing, and ... I forgot the pearls. *(They look at each other. Beat.)* Let's go. *(Linus takes Betsy by the hand and starts to walk out. Betsy doesn't quite know what to make of Linus' abruptness.)*

BETSY. What's the rush?

LINUS. I don't like good-byes, and I don't want to miss the Temple of Dendur. *(They walk out.)*

SCENE FOURTEEN

Linus and Betsy walk into the Temple of Dendur room in the Metropolitan Museum of Art. The Temple of Dendur is a magnificent Egyptian temple that was once on the bank of the Nile, but is now installed in the Met, surrounded by a wishing pool with many coins at its bottom.

LINUS. I used to come here all the time growing up, to think about stuff. Make wishes. *(Linus takes two pennies from his pocket and gives one to Betsy.)* Here. *(Linus and Betsy close their eyes, make wishes, and toss their pennies into the water.)*

BETSY. All those different wishes in there.

LINUS. I love wishes. The only reason to own a digital clock is when it's precisely 11:11, you get to make a wish.

BETSY. You do that?

LINUS. Ever since I was a little kid.

BETSY. Same with me.

LINUS. There's only two things you can trust in this world, 11:11 and the wishing pool at the Temple of Dendur. Nothing else works.

BETSY. What makes you so sure?

LINUS. God told me.

BETSY. Oh, God tells you things, does he?

LINUS. We were getting drunk in a bar one night and he confided in me.

BETSY. God drinks?

LINUS. He used to. He's in AA now. Or is it triple-A?

BETSY. That's cars.

LINUS. Right. He's in triple-A, too, in case his Jeep breaks. But AA really keeps him alive.

BETSY. "My name's God ... and I'm an alcoholic"?

LINUS. Yeah.

BETSY. So all that God Is Dead stuff was wrong? That's good to know.

LINUS. He was so upset by that whole thing. He wasn't dead, he was hungover. He just needed a *nap. (Beat.)* You're not tired, are you?

BETSY. Wide awake. Slept like a baby.

LINUS. Because we have a full night ahead of us.

BETSY. What's it full of?

LINUS. Spontaneity. That's all I claim to know.

BETSY. There's no plan, just go along for the ride?

LINUS. Yup. *(Beat.)* Okay, we didn't miss the Temple of Dendur. I had to see it, old time's sake, I've seen it, you've seen it, let's go.

BETSY. Are we going to be leaving every place in a hurry this evening?

LINUS. I told you, there's no plan.

BETSY. That's not true. Spontaneity is a plan.

LINUS. Well, aren't *we* a college student …

BETSY. What's that supposed to mean?

LINUS. I'll analyze my sentences back in California, there's no time for that sort of thing right now. We've got a town to paint. *(Linus starts to walk out. Betsy glances at the pennies in the water.)*

BETSY. I wonder if my wish will come true.

LINUS. What'd you wish for?

BETSY. Don't even try it. *(They walk out.)*

SCENE FIFTEEN

Linus and Betsy are standing on the Empire State Building's observation deck, looking out over Manhattan and beyond through the clear night air, at the lights and the birds flying around.

LINUS. Last time I was here, I got a nosebleed.

BETSY. No wonder.

LINUS.   I was doing lots of cocaine with Clyde. The view looks different when you're not so paranoid.

BETSY.   You can see *everything*.

LINUS.   Give me something to throw at the birds.

BETSY.   If you dropped a penny from up here and it hit somebody on the head, you think it would really drill a hole and kill them?

LINUS.   The bad news is, yes, it would kill them. The good news is, you'd get to make a wish.

BETSY.   I thought 11:11 and the Temple of Dendur were the only surefire wishes.

LINUS.   Yes, but it *also* works when you kill someone with a penny.

BETSY.   You and your wishes.

LINUS.   You made one, too.

BETSY.   Yes, but I didn't make a speech about God being an alcoholic.

LINUS.   He *is* an alcoholic. He's also a workaholic. I mean, six days to create the fucking *Earth?*

BETSY.   He made some mistakes.

LINUS.   He was *drunk. (Betsy laughs.)* What's so funny?

BETSY.   You. *(Beat.)* You are. Here we are, on top of the Empire State Building on a Saturday night, you're wearing a tuxedo and trying to tell me God's an alcoholic. I just ... find that funny. *(Betsy smiles at Linus. He smiles back and looks into her eyes.)*

LINUS.   Could you come here for a second?

BETSY.   Where?

LINUS.   Here. *(Betsy moves closer to Linus.)* Closer. *(Betsy moves closer.)* Closer. *(Betsy moves closer. She's very close to Linus now.)* Would you ask me to come closer to you and then kiss me, please?

BETSY.   *(Beat.)* Closer. *(Linus moves closer to Betsy and she kisses him, a tender first kiss.)*

LINUS.   Thanks. I hate making the first move, but I'm also impatient, so I —

BETSY.   Shhh ... *(Betsy kisses Linus for a long while.)*

LINUS. No matter how many times I do that, I'll always feel like I'm twelve. *(Excited, thrilled.)* Let's kiss for *hours*. Let's kiss till our lips hurt. *(They kiss for as long as it takes to make an average theater audience slightly uncomfortable.)*

SCENE SIXTEEN

Linus and Betsy are sitting at a table inside a 24-hour greasy spoon diner, glowing in their formal wear, looking totally out of place and yet also looking exactly right.

LINUS. Do you like kissing me?

BETSY. What kind of a question is that?

LINUS. I just want to make sure it was okay.

BETSY. How do *you* think it was?

LINUS. I think it was great.

BETSY. So what's the problem?

LINUS. I want to know if *you* think *I* was great.

BETSY. What do *you* think?

LINUS. I think I was exceptional.

BETSY. All men think they're great kissers, you know.

LINUS. But very few have a trophy to prove it.

BETSY. You don't have a kissing trophy.

LINUS. Sure I do. A little one. It's nothing much.

BETSY. If you've got a trophy, what do you need me for?

LINUS. You're prettier than my trophy. You kiss better, too. Your skin smells sweeter. Your hair wraps around my fingers — I mean, the trophy doesn't even *have* hair.

BETSY. You could buy a trophy wig. *(A Waitress comes over, pad and pencil in hand.)*

WAITRESS. What can I get for you tonight?

LINUS. Are you ready to order?

BETSY. Uhh, yes: I'll have ... a grilled cheese with tomato and a fruit salad.

WAITRESS. What kind of cheese?

BETSY.   Cheddar.

WAITRESS.   What kind of bread?

BETSY.   Whole wheat.

WAITRESS.   Anything to drink with that?

BETSY.   New Coke, please.

WAITRESS.   Excuse me?

BETSY.   New Coke.

WAITRESS.   We just have Coke.

BETSY.   Which kind?

WAITRESS.   Just Coke.

BETSY.   You don't know if it's Classic or New?

WAITRESS.   It's just Coke.

BETSY.   I'll have a lemonade, thank you.

WAITRESS.   And you?

LINUS.   7-Up.

WAITRESS.   Sprite okay?

LINUS.   Yeah, Sprite's okay, but I'd like a 7-Up.

WAITRESS.   We don't *have* 7-Up. Is Sprite okay?

LINUS.   Does it have the taste of Lymon?

WAITRESS.   It's Sprite. It's just *Sprite.*

LINUS.   Some Just Sprite, then. And, umm, let's see, a cheeseburger, medium rare, with feta cheese —

BETSY.   *Linus* ...

LINUS.   What?

BETSY.   Do you know how bad that is for you?

LINUS.   It tastes good.

BETSY.   Sure, it tastes good, but are you aware what you're putting into your body?

LINUS.   You washed down Valium with booze thousands of feet in the air and you're telling me to watch what I put in my body?

BETSY.   The heart attack unit at my father's hospital has never had a vegetarian come through its doors.

LINUS.   When I get back to California, I'll hire a vegetarian to come through its doors. But right now, I'll have a feta cheeseburger.

BETSY.   I won't kiss you.

LINUS.   *(To the Waitress.)* I'll have a grilled cheese on white bread with feta and tomatoes, a fruit salad, and a Sprite. How does that sound?

WAITRESS. Are you finished?

LINUS. I think so.

WAITRESS. That sounds good. *(The Waitress takes the menus and walks away.)*

LINUS. I hate peer pressure.

BETSY. Your heart will thank me.

LINUS. My taste buds will hold a grudge forever. *(Betsy leans over and kisses Linus.)* My taste buds would like you to know they officially forgive you.

BETSY. Oh, good.

LINUS. You taste sweet.

BETSY. Dessert from the wedding. Crème brûlée. You were talking to Clyde.

LINUS. I'm glad you came this weekend.

BETSY. You're a pretty great kisser. I just thought I should tell you.

LINUS. *(Obviously pleased.)* It takes two to tango.

BETSY. What does the tango have to do with us kissing?

LINUS. *(Slow, captivated.)* I don't know. All I know is … I got my wish.

SCENE SEVENTEEN

Betsy is sitting on Linus' bed, Linus is searching through a box of tapes.

LINUS. What was I thinking, listening to this stuff? I hate every tape I ever bought. Chicago Sixteen, Chicago Seventeen, Chicago Eighteen …

BETSY. Just put on the radio. *(Linus flips on the radio and searches for a station. A song like "Don't Cry Out Loud"* is playing.)*

---

* See Special Note on Songs and Recordings on copyright page.

LINUS. Suppress your emotions, *that's* a good message ... *(Linus turns the dial. A song like "Take Good Care of Yourself"* is playing, something overly possessive.)* A cheery song about slavery —

BETSY. It's not about slavery —

LINUS. It might as well be the theme song to *Roots. (Linus turns the dial. A Gregorian chant* is playing. Linus sits on the bed.)*

BETSY. What are you doing?

LINUS. I'm about to kiss you.

BETSY. You're not going to leave that on, are you?

LINUS. You don't find Gregorian chants romantic? *(Linus turns the dial. A song about "always loving" somebody, or "everlasting love," or "love forever" is playing.)* This should be illegal. There should be a law against these songs.

BETSY. I like this song.

LINUS. Oh, come on, you can't tell me you really *fall* for this. There should be somebody who tracks down songwriters who write songs about "everlasting always forever" love, and if they're not still in love with the person who inspired the song ten years later, they have to give back their royalties.

BETSY. They're singing what they *feel.*

LINUS. Most of them are lying.

BETSY. The songs might not be factual, but they're emotionally true. They're capturing the *feeling* of being in love.

LINUS. So they should sing "I *think* I'll always love you, I *hope* I always do, I know the statistics seem to indicate otherwise —" *(Linus turns the dial. A song like "Wonderful Tonight"* is playing.)* Now this, *this* is a song. You see, he's being positive, but he's realistic. Tomorrow, who knows? But *tonight* —

BETSY. *Tonight,* if you keep talking, will soon be tomorrow. *(Linus takes Betsy in his arms and kisses her with great passion. The song ends.)*

VOICE 4. This is Sy Covington, bringing you your favorite classic rock love songs this Saturday night on WCLS, the home of classic rock in New York City. *(Another song starts to play. Linus breaks from the kiss.)*

---

* See Special Note on Songs and Recordings on copyright page.

LINUS. Remember when "classic rock" was just *rock?*

BETSY. Yeah. *(Beat.) Yeah. (Betsy kisses Linus.)* I loved having you read me to sleep last night.

LINUS. I have a few talents. Kissing, directing films, reading to girls named Betsy at bedtime …

BETSY. My father reads my mother to sleep. She told me that's why she fell in love with him.

LINUS. Are your folks still together?

BETSY. Yeah.

LINUS. Are they happy?

BETSY. Yeah. Yeah, they are. I think they're the happiest married couple I've ever seen.

LINUS. Why? I mean, what do you think they *do…?*

BETSY. They're kind to each other. They're polite with each other. They still *like* each other. It's pretty weird.

LINUS. Does your father still read to your mother?

BETSY. Every night. She falls asleep with her head on his chest.

SCENE EIGHTEEN

Linus' bedroom. Later that night. Betsy is asleep with her head on Linus' chest. Linus is wide awake. After a moment, Linus moves, which wakes Betsy up.

BETSY. What's wrong?

LINUS. Nothing. I can't sleep.

BETSY. Why not?

LINUS. It's — I'm not really — I don't fall asleep when I'm in bed with somebody. It's … difficult. I need *I Love Lucy* beds …

BETSY. Should I sleep in the living room or something?

LINUS. No, no, I *want* you to sleep with — I want — I don't *know* what I want. I — it's just that — you know, *Robin* used to fall asleep exactly like you. Head in the same place, same exact thing.

BETSY. I'm sorry —

LINUS. It's not your fault. It's just — I shouldn't — I woke you up, I'm sorry —

BETSY. That's okay. I'm up. I'm up now. What's wrong?

LINUS. It's just that — when Robin and I first fell in love, you know, it was a big deal. I mean, she was really *it*. My first love, big stuff, earth shaking stuff. I could never fall asleep with her in my bed. So, you know, I'd just stay awake all night, staring at this beautiful creature in my arms, wondering what I did to deserve such luck. I would always be a zombie the next day, I had to take naps all the time, I felt like I was five years old again, but it didn't matter, it was worth it, just to watch my princess sleep every night. *(Beat.)* And then, one day, it wasn't worth it. I'd leave at night, go back to my dorm room, get a full night's sleep. The romance, the thrill, the excitement, it had all dulled a little, and all that was left were these two *people* — me over here, sleeping in one bed, her over there, sleeping in another, and for the first time there was this space in between, separating us. No matter how hard I tried, she was too far away.

BETSY. You really miss her.

LINUS. Yeah. She was my first love, you know, like I said. Yeah, I miss her … *God.*

BETSY. What?

LINUS. You know, I kiss Robin, I sleep with Robin, I grow distant from Robin, I kiss somebody else, I sleep with them, I never want to see them again, and then here I am, kissing you, sleeping with you — you know, sleeping *near* you — and, you know, is it just going to follow the pattern? Am I some romantic Flying Dutchman? How can I *know?*

BETSY. *(Casual.)* You *don't* know. You *shouldn't.* You shouldn't know *anything.* You're not *supposed* to. Love isn't *facts*, Linus. It isn't *knowledge.* If it was, you know, it would be *known* and people would say "I've fallen in knowledge" and it would be boring and we'd all find something else to do.

LINUS. *(Beat.)* Do you think it's easier for fortune tellers to fall in love? Since they know what's going to happen?

BETSY. I don't believe in fortune tellers.

LINUS.   I wish I did.
BETSY.   You can't wish.
LINUS.   Why not?
BETSY.   It's not 11:11. *(Betsy points to the alarm clock.)* See?

SCENE NINETEEN

Airplane. Linus and Betsy are sitting next to one another.

LINUS.   Now, hold on a second, let me get this straight: Love isn't knowledge, but it is ... an *airplane?*
BETSY.   *(Playful.)* Sort of.
LINUS.   First Pat Benatar says it's a battlefield, now you say it's an *airplane?* Love's an *airplane?*
BETSY.   Yeah, *sort* of ...
LINUS.   *Love. Is. An. Airplane.*
BETSY.   All I'm saying is it might be. You made a decision by getting on this plane, right? You wanted to get someplace. You might have had more freedom, in a way, by staying on the ground. But you might not end up getting where you wanted to go.
LINUS.   What if I get on the plane, but decide halfway through the trip I want to be on the ground?
BETSY.   There are parachutes, *risky* parachutes. But if you didn't *want* to get off — if you were enjoying the ride, you could stay on — you could become a pilot.
LINUS.   And you could become a stewardess.
BETSY.   Or I could become a pilot, and you could become a steward.
LINUS.   No, I'd want to be a stewardess, so I could wear a skirt.
BETSY.   You should have said "I'm joking" after that one ... *(Linus stares at Betsy for a beat. Then.)*
LINUS.   So, let me get this straight. Bear with me for a moment. The plane ride — that's like, marriage, or at least some

sort of commitment. The ground — no plane ride — that's, like, little journeys, total freedom, not a lot of distance covered. And pilots stand for lifetime monogamy. Did I get all the symbols?

BETSY.   Yes, you're very clever, you get a little silver star.

LINUS.   I want a gold star.

BETSY.   Tough luck, pal. You get a gold star when you get the moral behind the symbols. What am I saying? Big Picture Time.

LINUS.   Something about airplanes.

BETSY.   *Make a choice.* Who knows which? Who cares? Catch a later flight, get off the airplane at the airport, go straight back to where you came from. But you've got to know what you want. Don't act like you're flying when you're really walking, or walking when you're really flying, or walking and flying at the same time …

LINUS.   But I'm a Gemini.

BETSY.   I'm a Pisces, Linus, that doesn't mean I'm a *fish.*

LINUS.   Did you take some sort of *course* in all of this?

BETSY.   No, I just think about it … all the time.

LINUS.   I didn't realize how important airplanes were in your life.

BETSY.   Not just airplanes. You can turn almost anything into a metaphor for love.

LINUS.   You think airplane food can be a metaphor for love?

BETSY.   Absolutely not.

VOICE 2.   If you look towards the screen in the front of your cabin, we will now be showing a preview of our in-flight movie feature.

VOICE 3.   Gatorade Tarkington from the Dallas Cowboys is Romeo, a patriotic cop who's starting to lose hope.

LINUS.   This is one of my films. I'm very proud of it.

BETSY.   You could never make a movie like that.

LINUS.   Why not? I thought my choice was whatever I made it.

BETSY.   It's just not *you.*

LINUS.   What's *me,* then?

BETSY.   Well, I only saw *First Kiss* —

LINUS.   You only saw one short film and yet you're ready to *define* me and my work. I swear, everybody's a critic. Let's hear it. What's *me?*

BETSY.   Well, you seem to be all about going to these ridiculous lengths to manufacture romance. I mean, there's a man and he wants to sweep this woman off her feet, but it's almost the whole process that turns him on, rather than the woman herself. She could almost be an object, as long as he could still play the game, complete the chase. It's romantic, but there's room for growth.

LINUS.   *(Beat.)* Right.

BETSY.   What's wrong?

LINUS.   Oh, nothing, nothing …

BETSY.   Are you sure?

LINUS.   No, yeah, it's just that … I've been … I was thinking about this new film I've been putting together —

BETSY.   You didn't tell me you were doing a new film.

LINUS.   Yeah, well, that's — you know, I'm a film student, I'm usually doing a new film.

BETSY.   What's it about?

LINUS.   Well, it's — uhh, it's about this guy … and he's writing a love letter to his girlfriend on her birthday. She's 3000 miles away, on the other side of the country. He decides to write the love letter in longhand, 'cause it's more romantic. But his pencil breaks. He tries five pencils. They all break. So he writes the letter in his own blood. *(Beat.)* He goes to send it Federal Express. But he gets to the office four minutes late, and it's closed. He's a very superstitious guy, great believer in fate, and he takes the broken pencils and the closed Fed-Ex office as *signs,* he realizes he has to see her, he has to bring the letter to her by hand. So he books a flight. *(Beat.)* But the plane runs out of fuel and has to make a splash landing. Luckily, he survives, but his wallet is nowhere to be found. So he tries to call his girlfriend, but her answering machine picks up. She's *out.*

BETSY.   Where is she?

LINUS.   *Not home.* So he breathes deeply and starts to walk. *(Beat.)* He walks to her door, sits on her porch, waiting. *(Beat.)*

Finally, she arrives home. They embrace. He gives her the letter, and she is moved. The guy just wants to put the day's troubles behind him and settle in for a romantic evening with his love. They try to put on some romantic music, but her stereo is broken. So, even though the stove doesn't work, and they don't have a lighter or any matches, they manage to light a candle with the help of two twigs ... and a magnifying glass.

BETSY.   How is there sunlight during the evening?

LINUS.   ... A sun lamp is involved, okay? The guy's girlfriend is, like, the tan-obsessed daughter of George Hamilton. The point is, forget the problems and the hassles, because these two are together and they're in love. They set the candle on the bedside table and go about their naughty business. Unfortunately, they go about their business with a little too much zest.... *Vigor?... Zest....* And they knock the bedside table over, so the candle drops to the floor and sets the rug on fire. *(Beat.)* And then there's this neat effect that makes the film look like it's burning up, and after that come the closing credits. *(Beat.)* It's called *Burning Desire. (Beat.)* You don't think I'm too predictable, do you?

BETSY.   I think ... you're *adorable.*

LINUS.   But you're totally right about my films —

BETSY.   Like I said, there's room for growth, and when you're ready to grow, you will. But I'm only talking about your stuff because there's something good there already. There's room for growth in *everything.* That's not a bad thing.

LINUS.   You make me feel better than I did before I knew you.

BETSY.   Same here. Ditto. You know what I mean.

LINUS.   But, you know, I felt the same way about Robin at first.

BETSY.   I'm not her, Linus. I'm not a variation on some theme. I'm a whole different composer. Sure, there are going to be things in common. Mozart had ears. Bach had ears. Mozart put notes down on paper. So did Bach. But listen to the music, Linus. Listen to what each one *wrote.*

LINUS.   This whole metaphor thing is getting way out of

hand, Betsy. First the planes, now dead music guys — is there anything that *isn't* like something else, that's just ... *itself?*

BETSY.   *(Beat.)* When do you have to be back at school?

LINUS.   Tomorrow afternoon.

BETSY.   Do you feel like taking a drive when we get home?

LINUS.   Where?

BETSY.   You'll see.

SCENE TWENTY

A beautiful, expensive, tastefully decorated house on the beach in Malibu Colony at sunset. Betsy walks in the front door, followed by Linus, who shuts the door behind him.

LINUS.   Whose place is this?

BETSY.   Mine. My family's.

LINUS.   Not bad.

BETSY.   It's my favorite place in the world. Follow me. *(Linus follows Betsy as she walks through the house. She reaches some glass doors and opens them, and we are outside on the deck. Nothing comes between Linus and Betsy and the vastness of the Pacific Ocean but a thin strip of sand.)*

LINUS.   Oh, wow.

BETSY.   *This. (Beat.)* This isn't like anything else. This is just ... *this.*

LINUS.   I'd love to shoot a film here —

BETSY.   Don't film it, just ... just be here.

LINUS.   Yeah. *(Beat.)* Still, it'd be great to shoot a film here. *(Beat.)* It's just ... *amazing.*

BETSY.   Infinite possibilities. *(Beat.)* Sometimes, when I was younger, I'd be walking around here during the day, giggling with my friends or talking on the phone or watching TV, and my *father* would tell me that this place was special, that I should be careful not to waste my time here. He wanted me to take advantage of it, not to miss out on it when I was young. *(Beat.)* I think that's why he got it in the first place.

LINUS.   I wish I had known you when you were a little girl. I wish I knew what you were like.

BETSY.   We have pictures. I'll show you. *(Long silence. They both look out at the ocean. Betsy loves it, of course, but she's seen it before. Linus is captivated by it, since he's visiting. It's precious. Beat.)* I'm going into the bedroom. Want to come?

LINUS.   Yes. *(They kiss.)* I'll be there in a second. *(Betsy walks inside. Linus stares off at the ocean, which is filled with so many choices, perhaps too many for a confused young man who's fully aware that one day he will be gone.)*

BETSY.   *(Offstage. Pause.)* Linus ...

LINUS.   I'll be there in a second.

BETSY.   *(Offstage. Long pause.)* Linus ...

LINUS.   Be there in a second.

BETSY.   *(Offstage. Very long pause.)* Linus, are you coming in?

LINUS.   Be there in a second ...

BETSY.   *(Offstage. Extremely long pause.)* Linus...?

LINUS.   Be there in a second ... *(Linus stays put, not moving, staring out at the ocean with a blank look on his face, paralyzed.)*

END OF PLAY

47

PROPERTY LIST

Back pack (LINUS)
Video camera (BETSY)
Wire rim, blue glass, sunglasses (BETSY)
2 plane tickets (LINUS)
Large purse (BETSY)
Book *Letters to a Young Poet,* by Rilke (BETSY)
Photograph (LINUS)
Tuxedo (LINUS)
Business card (LINUS)
T-shirt (BETSY)
Boxer shorts (BETSY)
5 formal dresses on hangers (LINUS)
Teddy bear (BETSY, LINUS)
Spoon (LINUS)
Drinking glass (LINUS)
Drinking glasses with drinks (CLYDE, LINUS)
Pack of rolling papers (CLYDE)
Small bag of marijuana (CLYDE)
Marijuana joint (CLYDE)
Bottle of Visine (CLYDE)
Bottle of Binaca (CLYDE)
Shirley Temple drink (LINUS)
2 pennies (LINUS)
Pad and pencil (WAITRESS)
Menus (WAITRESS)
Box of cassette tapes (LINUS)

SOUND EFFECTS

Phone ringing

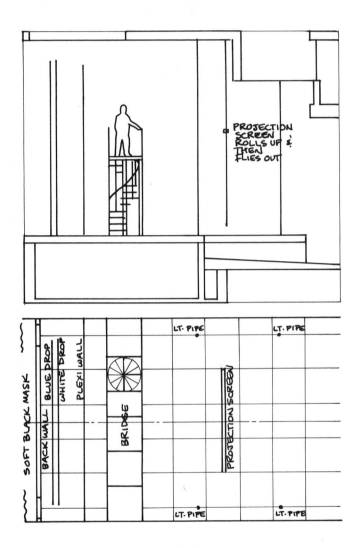

PROJECTION
SCREEN
ROLLS UP &
THEN
FLIES OUT

SOFT BLACK MASK

BACK WALL

BLUE DROP

WHITE DROP

PLEXI WALL

BRIDGE

PROJECTION SCREEN

LT. PIPE

LT. PIPE

LT. PIPE

LT. PIPE

SCENE DESIGN

"WONDERFUL TIME"

(DESIGNED BY HENRY DUNN FOR WPA THEATRE)